# DIGESTION AND REPRODUCTION

**Please visit our web site at: www.garethstevens.com**
**For a free color catalog describing Gareth Stevens Publishing's list**
**of high-quality books and multimedia programs, call 1-800-542-2595**
**or fax your request to (414) 332-3567.**

The editor would like to extend special thanks to Ronald J. Gerrits, Ph.D.
(Physiology), Medical College of Wisconsin, Milwaukee, Wisconsin, for his kind
and professional help with the information in this book.

**Library of Congress Cataloging-in-Publication Data**

Llamas, Andreu.
    [Digestión y la reproducción. English]
    Digestion and reproduction / by Andreu Llamas; illustrated by Luis Rizo.
       p.  cm. — (The human body)
    Includes bibliographical references and index.
    Summary: Describes the organs and their actions that are involved in the journey
of food through the body and the acts of ovulation, fertilization, and reproduction.
    ISBN 0-8368-2111-4 (lib. bdg.)
    1. Digestion—Juvenile literature.  2. Reproduction—Juvenile literature.
[1. Digestion.  2. Digestive system.  3. Reproduction.]  I. Rizo, Luis, ill.  II. Title.
III. Series: Llamas, Andreu. The human body.
QP145.L5813   1998
612.3—dc21                                                    98-16719

First published in North America in 1998 by
**Gareth Stevens Publishing**
A World Almanac Education Group Company
330 West Olive Street, Suite 100
Milwaukee, WI  53212  USA

This U.S. edition © 1998 by Gareth Stevens, Inc.
Original edition © 1996 by Ediciones Lema, S. L., Barcelona, Spain.
Additional end matter © 1998 by Gareth Stevens, Inc.

U.S. series editor:  Rita Reitci
Editorial assistant:  Diane Laska

Printed in Mexico

2 3 4 5 6 7 8 9 06 05 04 03 02

## Gareth Stevens Publishing
A WORLD ALMANAC EDUCATION GROUP COMPANY

# The Teeth

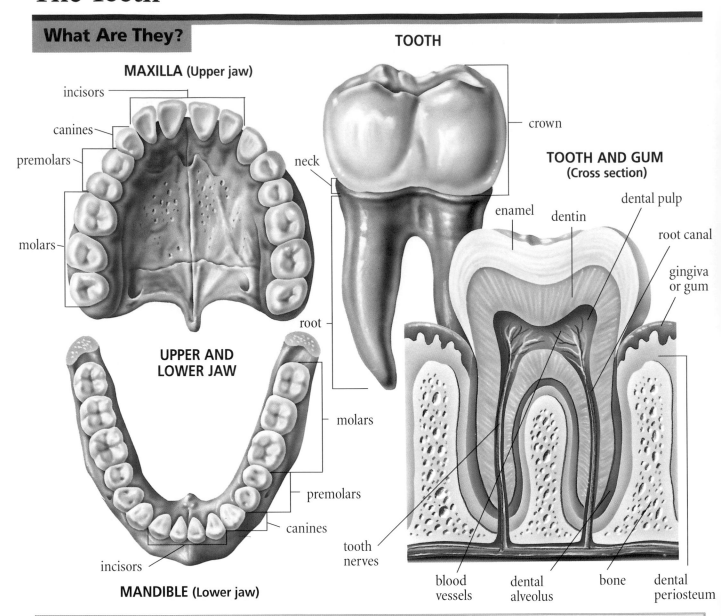

**MAXILLA (Upper jaw)**
- incisors
- canines
- premolars
- molars

**UPPER AND LOWER JAW**

**MANDIBLE (Lower jaw)**
- molars
- premolars
- canines
- incisors

**TOOTH**
- crown
- neck
- enamel
- root

**TOOTH AND GUM (Cross section)**
- dental pulp
- root canal
- gingiva or gum
- dentin
- tooth nerves
- blood vessels
- dental alveolus
- bone
- dental periosteum

The teeth in the upper and lower jaws physically break up food in the first stage of digestion to prepare it for passage through the digestive tract. Powerful muscles move the lower jaw, or mandible, while chewing food.

Every tooth has three main parts: root, neck, and crown. The root is the part inside the jaw's tooth socket, or dental alveolus. Here, tissue with nerves, blood capillaries, and fibers support the tooth. The neck of the tooth is a narrow connection between the root and the crown. The neck is covered by the gum, which is formed of mucous tissue with multiple blood vessels. The crown is the part of the tooth that stands out above the gum, or gingiva. Each crown provides a surface for processing food. Each tooth is shaped for a particular function.

Every tooth has layers of enamel, dentin, and pulp. Dentin, a type of bony tissue, forms most of the body of the tooth. The dentin of the crown is covered with enamel, the hardest substance in the body, made almost entirely of minerals. The root of the tooth is covered with a thin layer of bonelike tissue called cementum, produced by the dental periosteum. A space inside the dentin is filled with dental pulp, a sensitive tissue containing blood vessels and nerves.

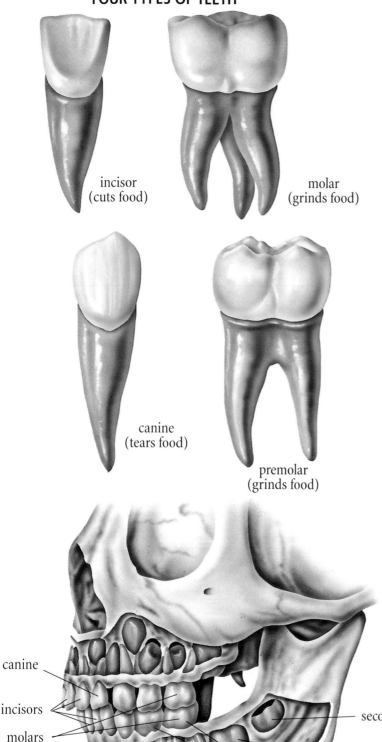

incisor
(cuts food)

molar
(grinds food)

canine
(tears food)

premolar
(grinds food)

canine

incisors

molars

second permanent molar

first permanent molar

molars

permanent teeth

**FORMATION OF PERMANENT TEETH
UNDERNEATH MILK TEETH**

**Types of teeth.** The act of chewing food provides a greater surface for digestive enzymes to attack in order to break down food molecules. To chew various foods, there are four kinds of teeth: incisors, canines, premolars, and molars. The upper and lower jaws have four incisors each. These have just one root and a sharp crown to cut the food. Each jaw has two canines, or eyeteeth. These have a single root and a sharp crown to tear food.

Both jaws possess four premolars, each with one or two roots. These teeth have cuboid crowns that reduce food to small particles. There are 12 molars altogether, shaped for grinding. The last molars are called wisdom teeth because they erupt during the "wise" years between ages 20 and 30. Many people do not ever have wisdom teeth.

**The first teeth.** Milk teeth, or deciduous teeth, start erupting between ages six months and eight months. In the following two or three years, 20 more teeth erupt — eight incisors, four canines, and eight molars. Starting around six years of age, the deciduous teeth are gradually replaced by permanent teeth. There are 32 permanent teeth in all. None are replaced with natural teeth if lost.

# The Salivary Glands and Tongue

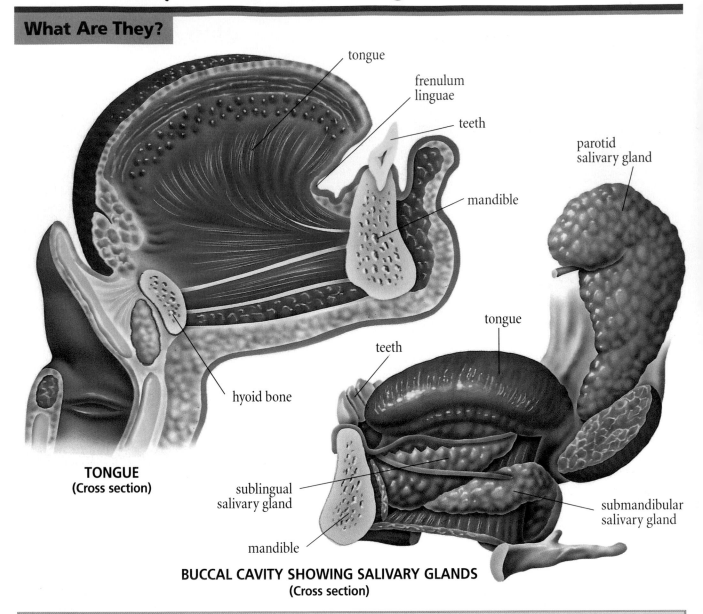

tongue

frenulum
linguae

teeth

parotid
salivary gland

mandible

tongue

teeth

hyoid bone

**TONGUE**
**(Cross section)**

sublingual
salivary gland

submandibular
salivary gland

mandible

**BUCCAL CAVITY SHOWING SALIVARY GLANDS**
**(Cross section)**

**Entering the body.** The buccal cavity houses the tongue, salivary glands, and teeth. The tongue, the biggest organ in the mouth, is formed from muscles. It has the remarkable ability to move in all directions because it is fixed at only two points.

The tongue muscles attach to the hyoid. The hyoid is a U-shaped bone at the back of the tongue, fastened to the skull by ligaments. The second attachment of the tongue is to the floor of the mouth with a flap of tissue called the frenulum linguae.

The buccal cavity holds three pairs of salivary glands: parotid (below and in front of the ears), sub-mandibular (below the mandible), and sublingual (under the tongue). The parotid glands are the largest. Salivary glands secrete saliva into the mouth, where it dissolves and moistens food, keeps the lips and tongue moist, and cleans the mouth of germs. The digestion process consists of reducing food to particles so small that eventually they can pass through the membranes of the intestines. Teeth do the mechanical work of grinding up food. The tongue mixes saliva into the food and starts the swallowing process. Saliva is mostly water, containing an enzyme called amylase that begins changing food starch into simple sugars.

# DIGESTIVE SYSTEM

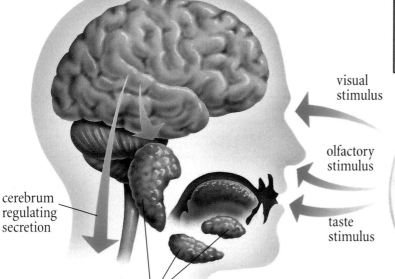

tongue
teeth
salivary gland
esophagus
passage of food
liver
gallbladder
large intestine
appendix
rectum
stomach
pancreas
small intestine
anus

**Saliva.** The saturation of food with saliva from chewing is called insalivation. While the teeth reduce the food to small particles, the tongue mixes in saliva. This moistens and softens the food, now called the alimentary bolus, for swallowing. The tongue starts the swallowing process by pushing the bolus to the back of the buccal cavity toward the pharynx.

The enzyme called amylase in saliva begins the digestive process. Amylase starts the chemical change of starch molecules into the simpler structures of glucose and maltose.

**Mouth watering.** The taste of food in the mouth increases salivary secretion. The sight or smell of food also increases salivation. These stimuli go to the brain, which interprets them and sends a signal to the salivary glands.

The amount of saliva secreted depends on the kind of food. For example, when you see a lemon, you probably start to secrete saliva. This is a defense mechanism to neutralize the acidity of lemon. Stress decreases salivation, making the mouth dry and swallowing difficult.

cerebrum regulating secretion

visual stimulus

olfactory stimulus

taste stimulus

salivary glands

## STIMULATION OF SALIVARY GLAND SECRETION

# The Pharynx, Esophagus, and Stomach

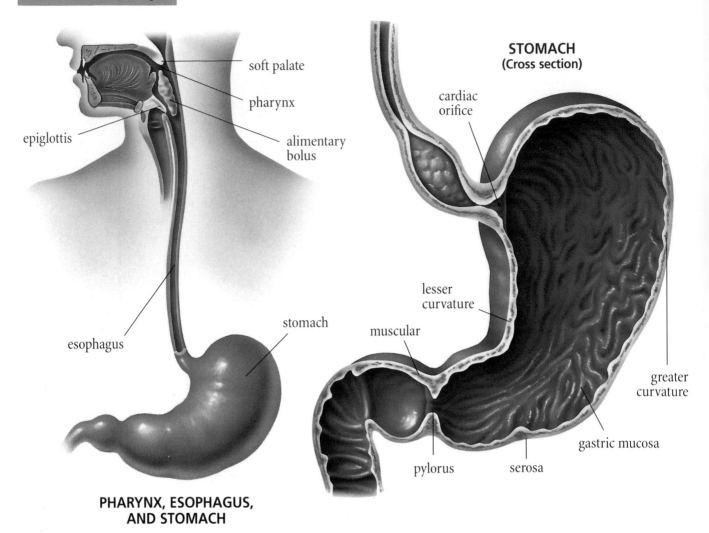

soft palate

pharynx

alimentary bolus

epiglottis

esophagus

stomach

**PHARYNX, ESOPHAGUS, AND STOMACH**

**STOMACH (Cross section)**

cardiac orifice

lesser curvature

muscular

greater curvature

gastric mucosa

pylorus

serosa

**Food tube.** The digestive system is also known as the digestive, or alimentary, tube because it is a tube 36 feet (11 meters) long. It starts in the mouth and ends in the anus. The alimentary bolus, when swallowed, reaches the stomach in a few seconds. It passes through the pharynx and down the esophagus, which is a tube about 10 inches (25 centimeters) long. The stomach is a strong muscular sac, in the shape of a **J**, nearly 8 inches (20 cm) long.

The stomach has an opening on each end. Food enters through the upper opening, or cardiac orifice. The lower opening, or pylorus, connects the stomach with the small intestine. The pylorus opens only after the gastric juices have transformed the bolus into substances ready for the action of the small intestine. Then the stomach uses one-way contractions, called peristaltic waves, to empty its contents by pushing the bolus through the pylorus into the small intestine.

The wall of the stomach has three layers: serosa, muscular, and gastric mucosa. The serosa is the outer membrane covering the entire stomach. The muscular layer is in the middle and is formed by three layers of muscles whose movements mix the alimentary bolus. The gastric mucosa lines the stomach. This membrane has numerous folds containing millions of gastric glands whose various secretions make up gastric juice. Digestion consists of the actions of these juices on the alimentary bolus.

Intake of air    Intake of food

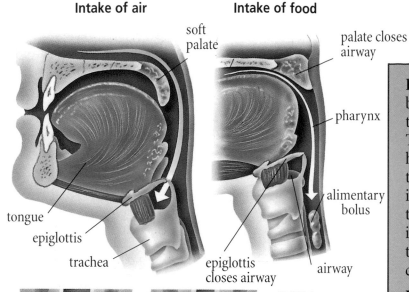

soft palate

palate closes airway

pharynx

alimentary bolus

tongue

epiglottis

trachea

epiglottis closes airway

airway

**Food or air.** When the tongue pushes the bolus toward the pharynx, structures in the pharynx guide it in the right direction. The movable soft palate at the back of the hard palate blocks the passage of food to the nasal fossae, or cavities. The epiglottis is a flap of tissue that blocks the airway to keep food out of the lungs and guide it into the esophagus. If some food goes the wrong way and into the airway, coughing expels it.

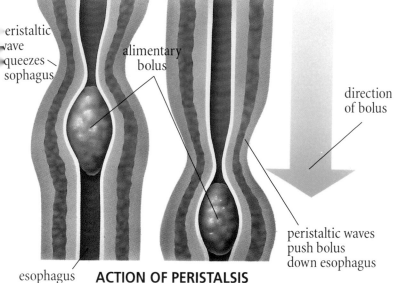

eristaltic wave queezes sophagus

alimentary bolus

direction of bolus

peristaltic waves push bolus down esophagus

esophagus    **ACTION OF PERISTALSIS ON FOOD**

**Peristalsis.** The muscular layer of the alimentary tube moves food with peristaltic waves (one-way contractions). These waves push the alimentary bolus down the esophagus into the stomach, then later out of the stomach into the small intestine. While food is in the stomach, the muscles churn it with gastric secretions into a liquid called chyme.

**Mixing.** Gastric juice is composed of hydrochloric acid, mucus, and an enzyme. Hydrochloric acid destroys most microorganisms that enter the stomach. It also helps activate the enzyme pepsin that changes proteins into amino acids. Mucus protects the stomach lining from the action of the acid. The sphincters, which are ringlike muscles, can close both ends of the stomach, keeping food for many hours and passing it gradually into the small intestine.

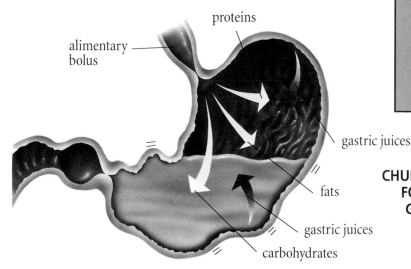

proteins

alimentary bolus

gastric juices

fats

gastric juices

carbohydrates

**CHURNING STOMACH MIXES FOOD PARTICLES WITH GASTRIC SECRETIONS**

# The Small Intestine

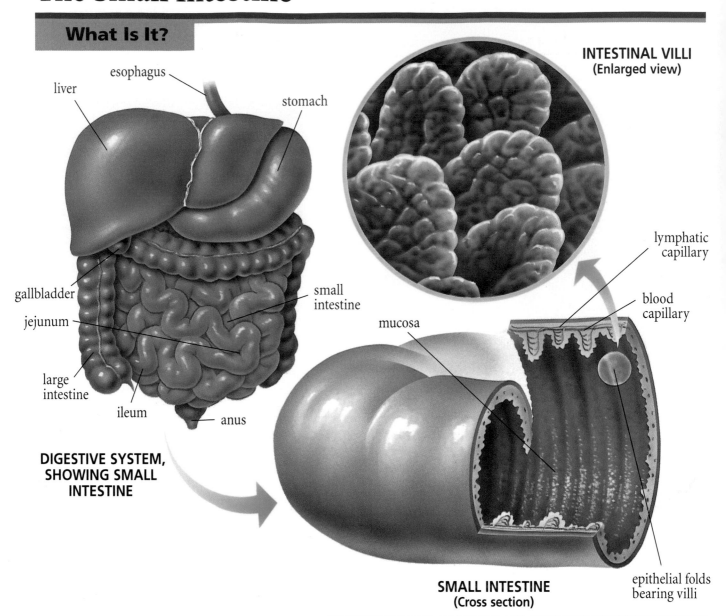

liver

esophagus

stomach

gallbladder

jejunum

small intestine

large intestine

ileum

anus

**DIGESTIVE SYSTEM, SHOWING SMALL INTESTINE**

**INTESTINAL VILLI**
**(Enlarged view)**

lymphatic capillary

blood capillary

mucosa

**SMALL INTESTINE**
**(Cross section)**

epithelial folds bearing villi

**The main site for digestion.** The body possesses two very different intestines — the large intestine and the small intestine. The small intestine is about 20 feet (6 m) long. It has a diameter of about 1 inch (2.5 cm). It reaches from the stomach to the large intestine. The small intestine is divided into the duodenum, jejunum, and ileum.

The duodenum, about 10 inches (25 cm) long, is the portion of the small intestine located immediately beyond the stomach. Its interior is completely lined with a mucous membrane, called the intestinal mucosa. The farther the mucosa is from the stomach, the more folds it has. The duodenum receives secretions from the pancreas (pancreatic juice) and from the liver (bile).

The jejunum and the thinner-walled ileum together make up most of the length of the small intestine. A microscopic view of the walls of the intestine shows a muscular layer lined with a folded mucosa. The surfaces of these folds are greatly increased by tiny projections called intestinal villi. Even the absorbing cells in the villi have microvilli to increase absorbing capacity. The small intestine secretes enzymes to complete digestion. Nutrients are then absorbed through intestinal villi into the capillaries and lymph vessels.

**INTESTINAL VILLI**

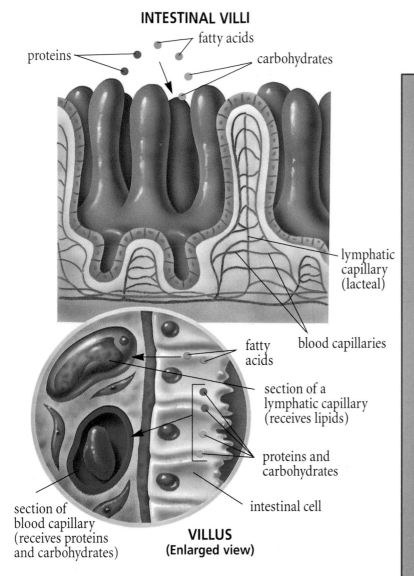

proteins

fatty acids

carbohydrates

lymphatic capillary (lacteal)

fatty acids

blood capillaries

section of a lymphatic capillary (receives lipids)

proteins and carbohydrates

intestinal cell

section of blood capillary (receives proteins and carbohydrates)

**VILLUS**
**(Enlarged view)**

**Intestinal villi.** Intestinal digestion takes place in the small intestine, and it depends on the actions of different juices — pancreatic secretions and bile secreted by the liver. These transform the chyme into a liquid containing very simple nutrients that can readily pass through the walls of the small intestine into the intestinal villi. Each villus contains blood capillaries to collect most of the nutrients, and lymphatic capillaries (lacteals) to collect fatty acids.

The passage through the small intestine lasts for hours. After being completely broken down and absorbed by the villi, each kind of nutrient goes a different way. Proteins and carbohydrates go to the liver, where they are stored. Fatty acids enter the lymphatic system.

**Chyme passes on.** When the contents of the stomach are too acid, the pyloric sphincter opens for a few seconds to allow some of the material into the duodenum.

There, it is mixed with secretions of the pancreas (which neutralize acidity) and the gallbladder. The digestive system contains "nervous" networks that control the intestinal movements and regulate the secretion of the different juices.

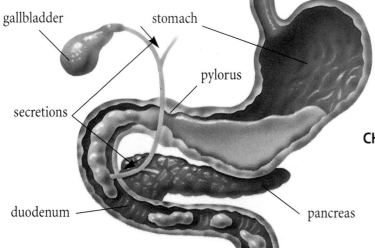

gallbladder

stomach

pylorus

secretions

duodenum

pancreas

**CHYME ENTERING DUODENUM**
**FOR FURTHER DIGESTION**

# The Liver

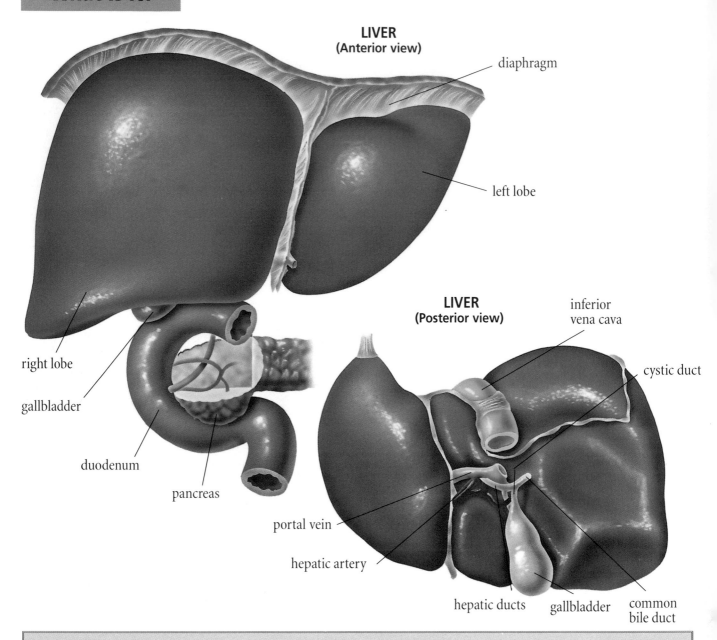

**LIVER**
(Anterior view)

diaphragm

left lobe

right lobe

gallbladder

duodenum

pancreas

**LIVER**
(Posterior view)

inferior vena cava

cystic duct

portal vein

hepatic artery

hepatic ducts

gallbladder

common bile duct

**The most vital organ.** The liver, located on the right side of the abdomen, under the diaphragm, is the biggest gland of the body. It weighs approximately 3.3 pounds (1.5 kilograms) and is about 8 inches (20 cm) long. Two membranes cover it, and the lower ribs protect it.

The liver is divided into five lobes. The right lobe is six times larger than the left lobe. Three smaller lobes — the quadrate, the Spigelian, and the caudate — are part of the right lobe. All nutrients from the intestines go to the liver. The liver warms the blood and heats the entire body. It makes proteins and many blood-clotting factors. It produces bile — and stores it in the gallbladder.

The liver stores a form of glucose and several types of vitamins. It also manufactures vitamin A. It breaks down alcohol and drugs, bacteria, old blood cells, toxins, and excess hormones. Damage to the liver can be very serious because this organ is extremely necessary to life.

**HEPATIC**
(Enlarged view)

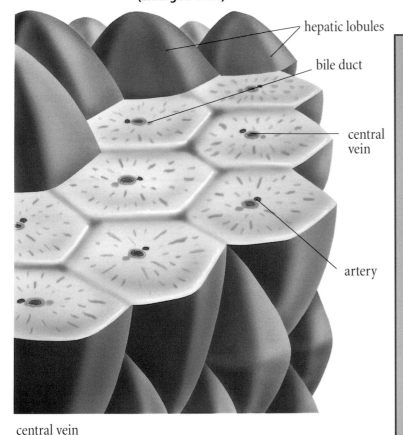

hepatic lobules

bile duct

central
vein

artery

central vein
(branch of portal vein)

bile duct

branch of portal vein

**HEPATIC LOBULE**

hepatic cells
(filter the blood)

hepatic artery

**Hepatic lobules.** The liver contains from 50,000-100,000 hepatic lobules, each 0.08-0.16 inch (2-4 millimeters) long and 0.04-0.08 inch (1-2 mm) in diameter. A lobule is shaped like a hexagon, and its numerous cells are surrounded by blood capillaries. All the blood from the intestines flows into the portal vein and then into the liver. At that point, the portal vein splits into smaller and smaller branches that end in the lobules. There, the hepatic cells secrete useful products into the blood. They also remove wastes and other substances from the blood.

The hepatic cells use old red blood cells to produce bile. This fluid breaks down fats into very small globules so that enzymes can act upon them. Bile is stored in the gallbladder until needed. Then it flows through the common bile duct to the duodenum, where the sphincter of Oddi regulates the flow of bile into the intestine.

Blood and bile circulate through different vessels and never mix. The liver can regenerate easily. But alcohol, drugs, and infections can seriously damage the liver and threaten life.

# The Gallbladder and Pancreas

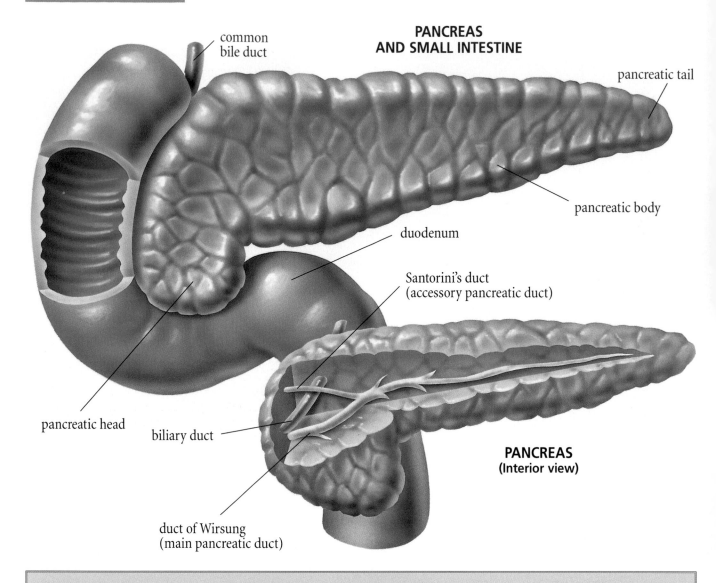

common
bile duct

PANCREAS
AND SMALL INTESTINE

pancreatic tail

pancreatic body

duodenum

Santorini's duct
(accessory pancreatic duct)

pancreatic head

biliary duct

PANCREAS
(Interior view)

duct of Wirsung
(main pancreatic duct)

**Gallbladder.** Bile made by the liver travels through hepatic ducts to be stored in the gallbladder. This is a small sac on the underside of the right lobe of the liver. It holds about 2 ounces (60 milliliters) of bile.

When chyme enters the duodenum, the gallbladder releases bile through the cystic duct, which joins the hepatic duct to form the common bile duct. This enters the duodenum at a bulge, called the ampulla of Vater, where bile flow is controlled by the sphincter of Oddi.

**Pancreas.** The pancreas is an elongated gland below the stomach. Pancreatic cells called acini produce pancreatic juice, which travels through Santorini's duct and the duct of Wirsung to enter the duodenum at the ampulla of Vater. The juice contains digestive enzymes. Pancreatic amylase changes starch to a simple sugar; trypsin changes proteins to short amino acids; and lipase changes fats to fatty acids and glycerol. Bile first breaks fats into tiny globules so lipase can work on them.

**Insulin.** Scattered through the pancreas are the islets of Langerhans, cells that secrete insulin into the blood. Insulin allows glucose to be changed into glycogen, which is stored in the liver and used as fuel for muscles when energy is needed.

## PANCREATIC CELLS

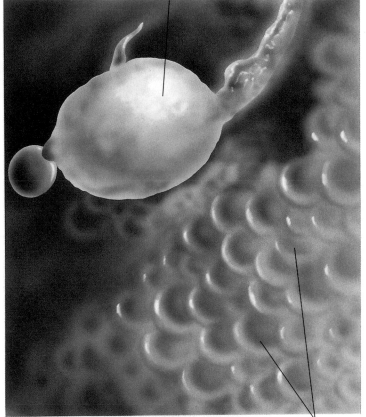

islets of Langerhans

acini cells produce enzymes

**Pancreatic cells.** In the pancreas, the islets of Langerhans secrete insulin into the blood. Pancreatic cells that are called acini produce digestive enzymes. The pancreas also produces bicarbonate juice to neutralize the acidic chyme in the duodenum.

**Bile.** Bile is a bitter, yellow fluid formed from water, bile salts, phospholipids, cholesterol, proteins, pigments, and ions, such as sodium. The liver produces over a quart (liter) of bile each day. The gallbladder removes water, concentrating the bile to one-tenth its volume.

Chyme in the small intestine triggers a release of bile. Bile salts break fat into tiny globules for digestion. The salts are then reabsorbed by the ileum and sent back to the liver to be reused.

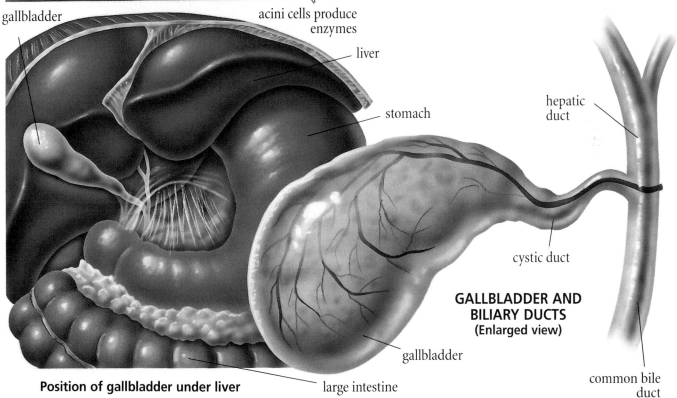

gallbladder

liver

stomach

hepatic duct

cystic duct

**GALLBLADDER AND BILIARY DUCTS**
(Enlarged view)

gallbladder

common bile duct

**Position of gallbladder under liver**

large intestine

# The Large Intestine

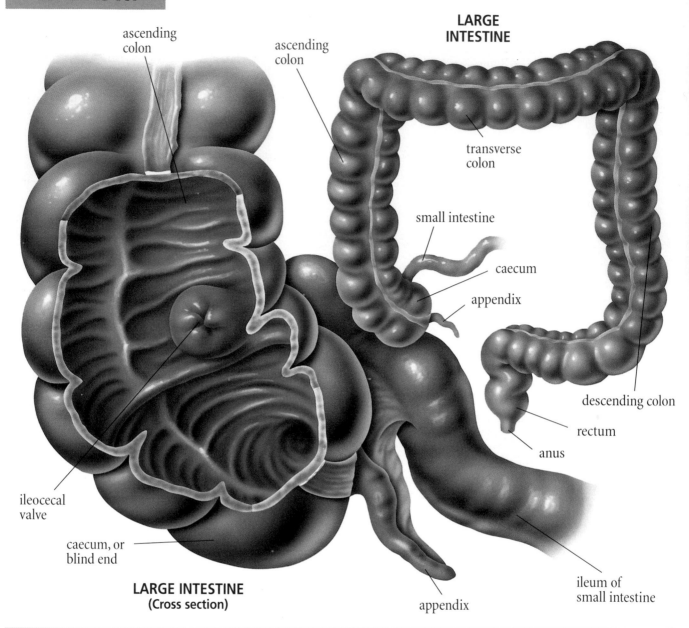

ascending colon

ascending colon

LARGE INTESTINE

transverse colon

small intestine

caecum

appendix

descending colon

rectum

anus

ileum of small intestine

ileocecal valve

caecum, or blind end

**LARGE INTESTINE**
**(Cross section)**

appendix

**Handling the leftovers.** The products which have not been absorbed by the villi of the small intestine pass into the large intestine through the ileocecal valve, forming a dense paste. The large intestine is only 5.3 feet (1.6 m) long, although it has a bigger diameter than the small intestine. It is divided into three main parts: caecum, colon, and rectum. The caecum is the first section of the large intestine. It bears the vermicular appendix, a short and narrow tube. When this tube is infected, the condition is known as appendicitis. The colon has three sections: ascending; transverse, from right to left; and descending, down to the pelvis. During the passage along the colon, water contained in the food is absorbed. Bacteria normally inhabiting the colon produce some vitamins the body needs. The rectum is the last portion of the digestive tract. It has a wide section, called the rectal ampulla, which narrows at the end. There, sphincters control the opening of the anus to expel the feces.

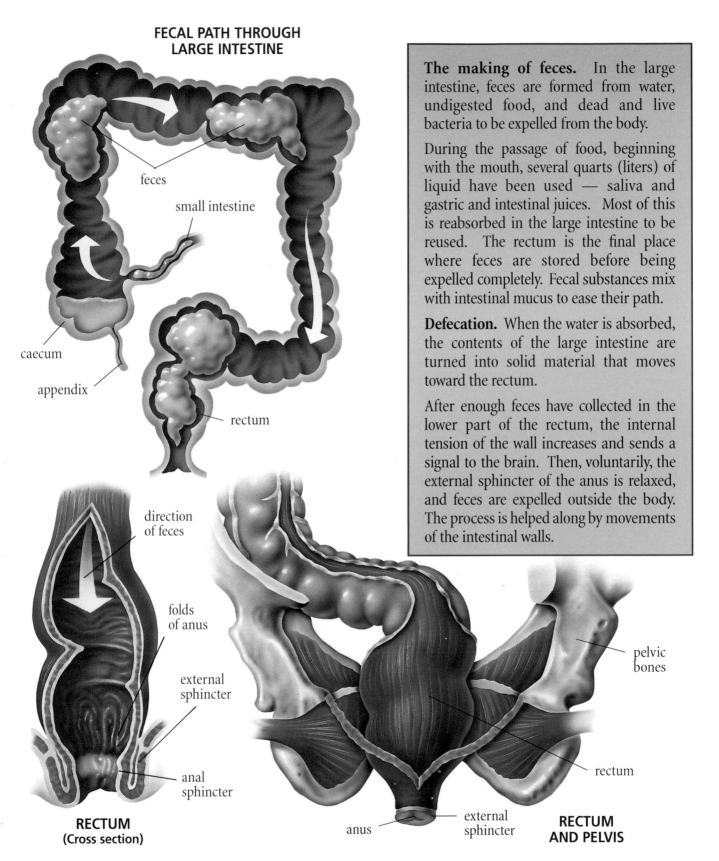

**FECAL PATH THROUGH LARGE INTESTINE**

feces

small intestine

caecum

appendix

rectum

**The making of feces.** In the large intestine, feces are formed from water, undigested food, and dead and live bacteria to be expelled from the body.

During the passage of food, beginning with the mouth, several quarts (liters) of liquid have been used — saliva and gastric and intestinal juices. Most of this is reabsorbed in the large intestine to be reused. The rectum is the final place where feces are stored before being expelled completely. Fecal substances mix with intestinal mucus to ease their path.

**Defecation.** When the water is absorbed, the contents of the large intestine are turned into solid material that moves toward the rectum.

After enough feces have collected in the lower part of the rectum, the internal tension of the wall increases and sends a signal to the brain. Then, voluntarily, the external sphincter of the anus is relaxed, and feces are expelled outside the body. The process is helped along by movements of the intestinal walls.

direction of feces

folds of anus

external sphincter

anal sphincter

**RECTUM**
(Cross section)

pelvic bones

rectum

anus

external sphincter

**RECTUM AND PELVIS**

# The Urinary System: The Kidneys

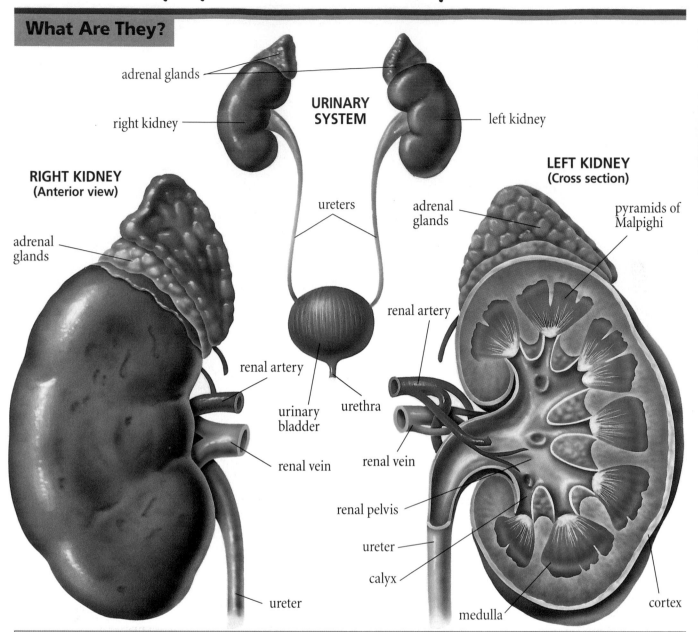

**URINARY SYSTEM**

adrenal glands

right kidney

left kidney

**RIGHT KIDNEY**
(Anterior view)

**LEFT KIDNEY**
(Cross section)

adrenal glands

pyramids of Malpighi

adrenal glands

ureters

renal artery

renal artery

urinary bladder

urethra

renal vein

renal vein

renal pelvis

ureter

calyx

ureter

cortex

medulla

**Getting rid of waste water.** The urinary system is composed of the kidneys and the urinary ducts. It filters the blood and retains water and waste from the body's metabolism, forming urine. This fluid travels through the ureters to the bladder, where it is stored until eliminated through the urethra.

The kidney of an adult weighs about 4-10.5 ounces (120-300 grams) and is about 4-5 inches (10-12 cm) long. A layer of fibrous tissue protects each kidney. Inside are the cortex and the medulla.

The yellow-brown cortex makes up the outer part of the kidney. The medulla is red and is shaped like pyramids (the pyramids of Malpighi). The apex of each pyramid, the papilla, points inward and forms the interior of the kidney.

The kidney pelvis connects with the ureter. The pelvis is a broad, funnel-shaped space formed by the junction of the ducts coming from the rest of the kidney. The pelvis collects the urine produced by the nephrons inside the kidney.

The nephron is the kidney's smallest functional unit. It is composed of a glomerulus and tubules surrounded by a capillary network. Each kidney has more than a million nephrons!

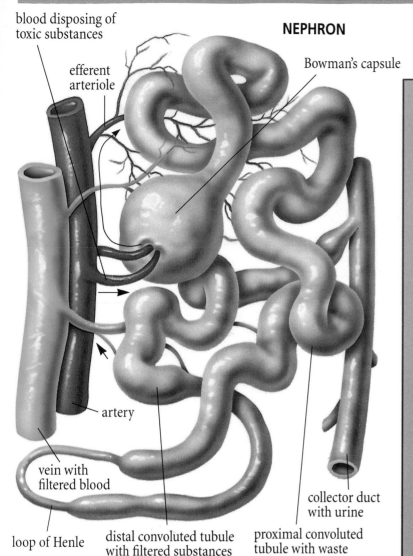

**NEPHRON**

blood disposing of toxic substances

efferent arteriole

Bowman's capsule

artery

vein with filtered blood

loop of Henle

distal convoluted tubule with filtered substances

proximal convoluted tubule with waste

collector duct with urine

**The nephron.** In the nephron, blood capillaries form a close knot, or glomerulus, which is surrounded by a membrane called Bowman's capsule. An afferent arteriole brings blood into Bowman's capsule, which removes some plasma and dissolved substances to form tubular fluid. An efferent arteriole carries blood out of the capsule, where it enters the peritubular capillaries, a network covering the entire nephron. From venous capillaries, the blood flows to the renal vein and travels to the vena cava near the heart.

From Bowman's capsule, the tubular fluid enters the collecting tubule. Different parts of the tubule reabsorb water and useful substances, which pass through the walls into the peritubular capillaries. Wastes and excess water continue as urine through the collecting ducts to the renal pelvis, a large opening that funnels the urine through the ureter to the bladder.

**Adrenal glands.** The human body has two adrenal glands — one on top of each kidney. The gland's outer layer, or cortex, produces cortisone, a hormone. The inner part, or medulla, produces adrenaline, another hormone.

Cortisone regulates the metabolism of carbohydrates, proteins, and fats. It maintains normal amounts of sodium and potassium in the blood, contributing to normal blood pressure, blood volume, and normal balance of acidity and alkalinity.

Adrenaline prepares the body to face dangerous situations. It temporarily stops digestion, raises the heart rate, and increases glucose in the blood to be used for extra energy.

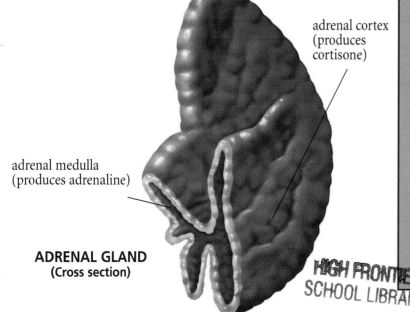

adrenal cortex (produces cortisone)

adrenal medulla (produces adrenaline)

**ADRENAL GLAND**
**(Cross section)**

**17**

# The Urinary System

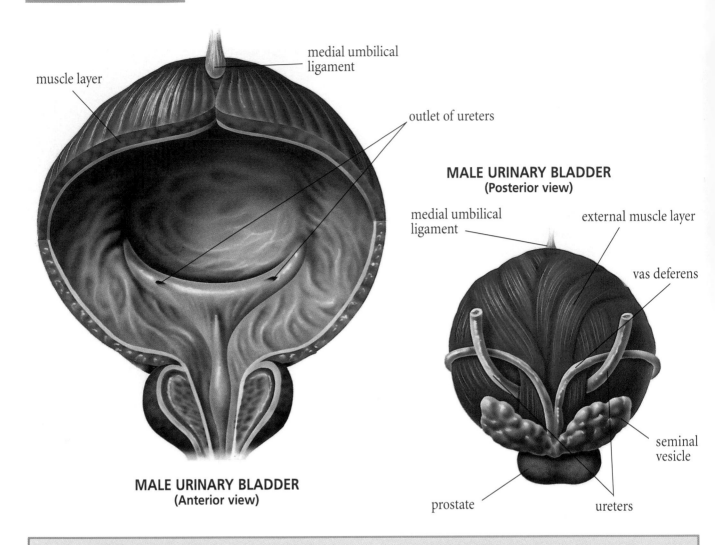

muscle layer

medial umbilical ligament

outlet of ureters

**MALE URINARY BLADDER**
(Posterior view)

medial umbilical ligament

external muscle layer

vas deferens

seminal vesicle

prostate

ureters

**MALE URINARY BLADDER**
(Anterior view)

**Ureters.** The ureters are two ducts about 10-12 inches (25-30 cm) long that carry urine from the kidneys to the bladder. Each of the ureters is formed by a continuation of the renal pelvis. The wall of the ureter has two different layers: a mucosa, which lines the interior; and the muscle layer, which allows the ureter to contract. These contractions propel the urine toward the bladder.

**Bladder.** The bladder looks like an elastic sac formed by muscle tissue. It is located behind the pubis in the lower abdomen. It stores the urine that reaches it through the ureters. Because of muscle tissue, the bladder can expand to store a fairly large amount of urine, almost half a quart (0.5 liter).

**Urethra.** The urethra is a duct that carries the urine from the bladder to the outside of the body.

The shape of the urethra is different according to sex, because of the presence of the reproductive organs. For example, in the male, the urethra is about 7-8 inches (18-20 cm) long. In the female, it is about 1.5 inches (4 cm) long.

**Urine.** Urine is composed of 95 percent water and 2 percent mineral salts. The remaining 3 percent is urea and uric acid — the forms in which nitrogen from protein metabolism is removed from the body. All the blood in the body circulates thirty times a day through the kidneys, where it is filtered.

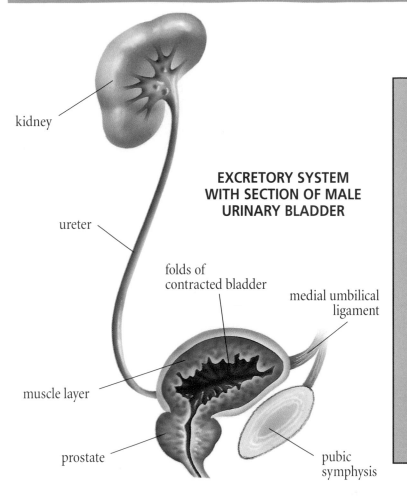

kidney

ureter

**EXCRETORY SYSTEM
WITH SECTION OF MALE
URINARY BLADDER**

folds of
contracted bladder

medial umbilical
ligament

muscle layer

prostate

pubic
symphysis

**Storing waste water.** The bladder stores urine with the help of two sphincters, the internal and the external. The internal sphincter is inside the bladder, around the opening of the urethra, and it works involuntarily. The external sphincter is in the urethra, about 0.8 inch (2 cm) below the internal sphincter, and it is under human control.

When the bladder is one-fourth to one-half full, a nerve impulse causes it to contract. At the same time, it relaxes the internal urethral sphincter. When a person voluntarily relaxes the external urethral sphincter, the bladder empties and urine flows out through the urethra. Humans can control the external urethral sphincter until the bladder is full.

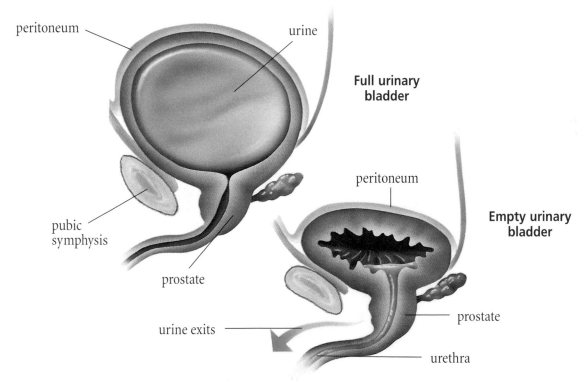

peritoneum

urine

**Full urinary
bladder**

pubic
symphysis

prostate

peritoneum

**Empty urinary
bladder**

urine exits

prostate

urethra

# The Male Reproductive System

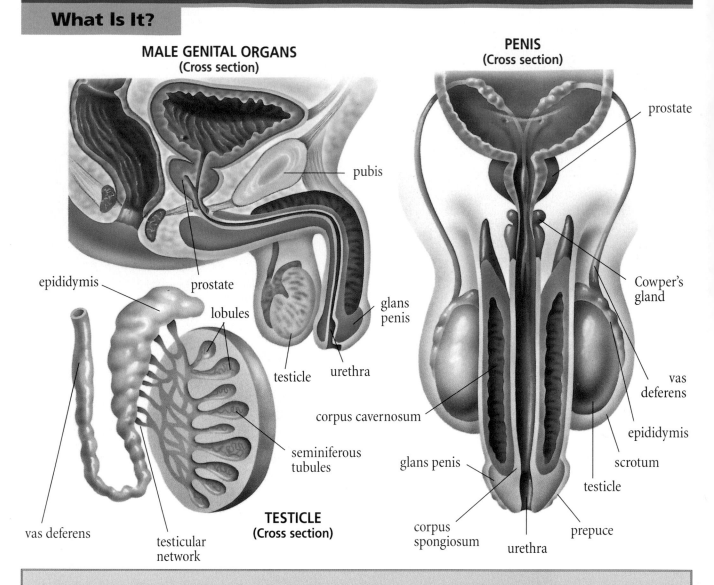

**MALE GENITAL ORGANS**
(Cross section)

**PENIS**
(Cross section)

pubis

prostate

epididymis

prostate

lobules

glans
penis

Cowper's
gland

testicle

urethra

corpus cavernosum

vas
deferens

seminiferous
tubules

epididymis

glans penis

scrotum

**TESTICLE**
(Cross section)

testicle

vas deferens

testicular
network

corpus
spongiosum

prepuce

urethra

**Testicles.** Testicles are what are known as male gonads. They consist of two oval glands 1.5-2 inches (4-5 cm) long, placed outside the abdominal cavity. They are protected by the scrotum, a pouch of skin that regulates the temperature of the testicles.

A testicle contains about 200-300 spermatic lobes. Each lobe has one to three very thin seminiferous tubules, about 12-28 inches (30-70 cm) long, which are extensively folded. These lead to the testicular network. The walls of the seminiferous tubules contain the germinal cells, which produce spermatozoa, the male reproductive cells.

From puberty on, the seminiferous tubules produce around 200 million spermatozoa daily. Each testicle also produces male sex hormones. Spermatozoa leave the testicle, traveling through a narrow duct to the epididymis, where they finish maturing. They then pass into the vas deferens, which joins the ejaculatory duct. The pair of ejaculatory ducts leads to the urethra that runs through the penis.

**Penis.** The penis is the male copulating organ. Inside it lie the corpora cavernosa, two smooth muscular masses situated above the urethra.

The urethra is surrounded by a spongy body, the corpus spongiosum, which widens at the end of the penis to form the glans penis. The outside of the glans is protected by a fold of skin, called the prepuce or foreskin.

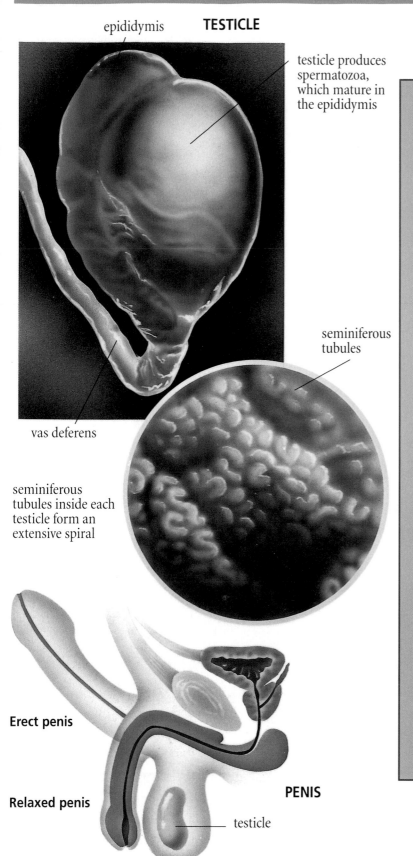

epididymis

**TESTICLE**

testicle produces
spermatozoa,
which mature in
the epididymis

seminiferous
tubules

vas deferens

seminiferous
tubules inside each
testicle form an
extensive spiral

Erect penis

Relaxed penis

**PENIS**

testicle

**Maturing sperm.** Spermatozoa mature for about 10 days inside the epididymis, which stores them in a duct more than 16 feet (5 m) long. Then, in order to complete the formation of semen, the seminal tubes receive secretions from various glands — the seminal vesicles and the prostate and Cowper's glands. The two seminal vesicles at the end of the vas deferens secrete a fluid containing fructose, a sugar that provides energy to the sperm. The fluid is alkaline to increase sperm mobility. The prostate gland lies at the beginning of the urethra, just below the bladder. It secretes a viscous alkaline fluid that ensures the mobility of sperm. Finally, two Cowper's glands pour an alkaline mucous secretion into the urethra, which completes the composition of semen.

**Semen.** Semen is expelled through the urethra, which also carries urine outside the body. During sexual intercourse between a man and a woman, the penis enters the vagina, or female reproductive organ, and ejaculates, or expels semen.

To make this possible, the penis must change from a relaxed state to a firm and erect position. Nerve impulses widen arteries to the penis, which then pour large amounts of blood into the sinuses, or cavities, of the corpora cavernosa and corpus spongiosum. This produces the firmness and upright position of the penis that enables intercourse to take place.

# The Spermatozoon

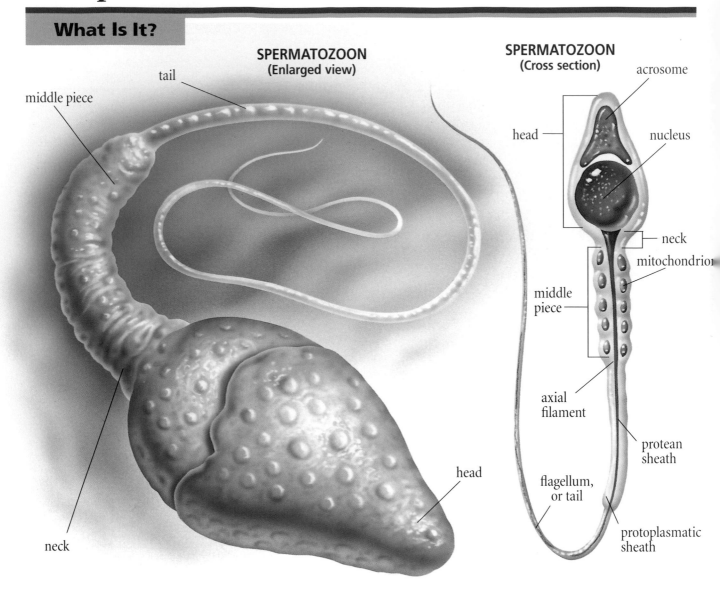

SPERMATOZOON
(Enlarged view)

tail

middle piece

neck

head

SPERMATOZOON
(Cross section)

acrosome

head

nucleus

neck

mitochondrion

middle piece

axial filament

protean sheath

flagellum, or tail

protoplasmatic sheath

**Producing male sex cells.** Spermatogenesis, the production of spermatozoa, takes place in the testicles. A mature testicle contains one billion spermatogonia, primary germinating cells that multiply, each developing into four spermatozoa. Around 200 million spermatozoa can be produced every day. Each spermatozoon is 0.002-0.0024 inch (50-60 microns) long and has four main parts: head, neck, middle piece, and tail. The head is the widest part of the cell, measuring about 0.00012-0.0002 inch (3-5 microns) long. The head contains the nucleus; in front of this lies the acrosome, a structure rich in energy that contains the enzymes needed by the spermatozoon to penetrate the membranes of the ovum. The neck is the short connection between the head and the middle piece. Inside, the neck produces the microfibrils of the tail.

The middle piece is 0.00024 inch (6 microns) long and contains a central axial filament, which is surrounded by mitochondria. These are minute cellular structures that provide the energy needed for the tail's movements.

The long, thin tail is formed from the axial filament, a protein structure. This is covered by a protoplasmatic sheath. The whiplike tail, or flagellum, propels the spermatozoon toward the ovum at a speed of 0.12 inch (3 mm) per minute.

## SPERMATOGENESIS

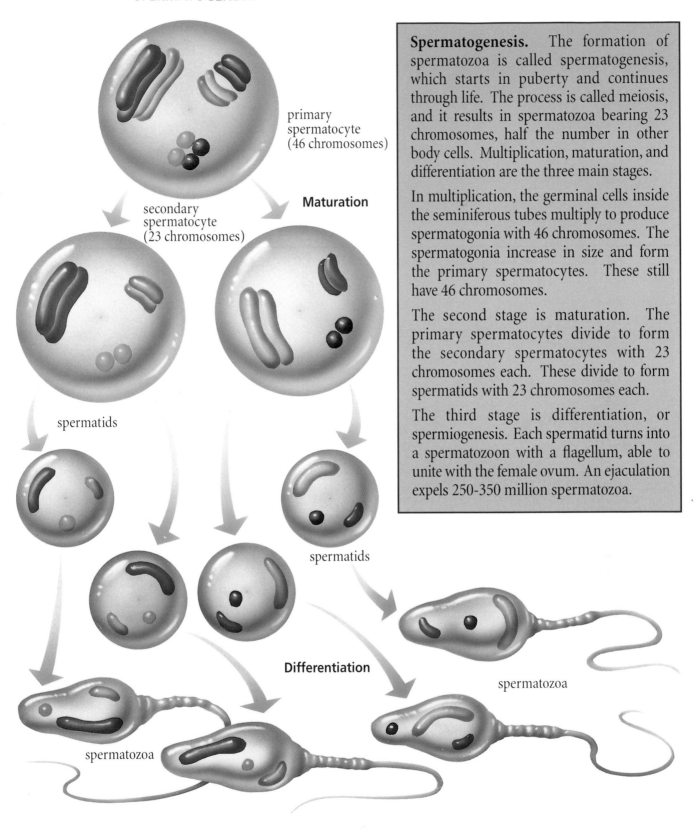

primary
spermatocyte
(46 chromosomes)

**Maturation**

secondary
spermatocyte
(23 chromosomes)

spermatids

spermatids

**Differentiation**

spermatozoa

spermatozoa

**Spermatogenesis.** The formation of spermatozoa is called spermatogenesis, which starts in puberty and continues through life. The process is called meiosis, and it results in spermatozoa bearing 23 chromosomes, half the number in other body cells. Multiplication, maturation, and differentiation are the three main stages.

In multiplication, the germinal cells inside the seminiferous tubes multiply to produce spermatogonia with 46 chromosomes. The spermatogonia increase in size and form the primary spermatocytes. These still have 46 chromosomes.

The second stage is maturation. The primary spermatocytes divide to form the secondary spermatocytes with 23 chromosomes each. These divide to form spermatids with 23 chromosomes each.

The third stage is differentiation, or spermiogenesis. Each spermatid turns into a spermatozoon with a flagellum, able to unite with the female ovum. An ejaculation expels 250-350 million spermatozoa.

# The Female Reproductive System

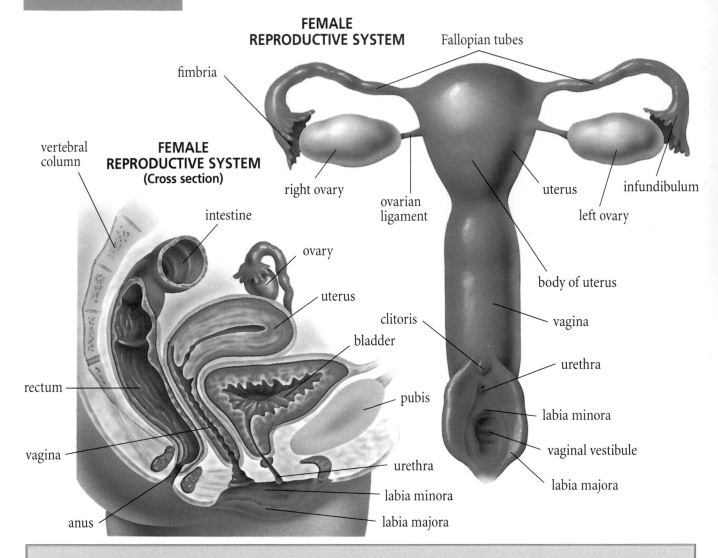

**FEMALE REPRODUCTIVE SYSTEM**

Fallopian tubes

fimbria

right ovary

ovarian ligament

uterus

infundibulum

left ovary

body of uterus

vagina

urethra

clitoris

labia minora

vaginal vestibule

labia majora

vertebral column

**FEMALE REPRODUCTIVE SYSTEM (Cross section)**

intestine

ovary

uterus

bladder

pubis

rectum

vagina

urethra

labia minora

anus

labia majora

**Female reproductive organs.** The reproductive system of the female consists of internal organs (ovaries, Fallopian tubes, uterus, and vagina) and external organs (labia majora and labia minora, clitoris, vaginal vestibule, and vestibular glands).

The two ovaries are the female gonads. They are oval shaped, placed in the lower abdomen, and measure about 1-2 inches (2.5-5 cm) long. Each ovary has a cortex and medulla. The cortex contains follicles, cavities that hold developing sex cells. The medulla consists of tissue plentifully supplied with blood vessels and nerves. Periodically, a mature follicle in the cortex opens to release an ovum, the female sexual cell. The remains of the follicle form the corpus luteum.

The Fallopian tubes, or oviducts, are about 4 inches (10 cm) long. A wide, funnel-shaped end, called the infundibulum, curves over the ovary. The other end of the oviduct attaches to the uterus.

The uterus is a hollow, muscular organ about 3 inches (8 cm) long. Periodically, the uterine mucosa prepares for the implantation of an ovum. It develops an endometrium, a thick spongy tissue with numerous blood vessels. There, the fertilized ovum, or zygote, implants and develops during the nine months of a pregnancy.

The upper uterus is called the uterine body. It is connected to the vagina by a short constriction called the neck, or cervix.

## OVARY
### (Cross section)

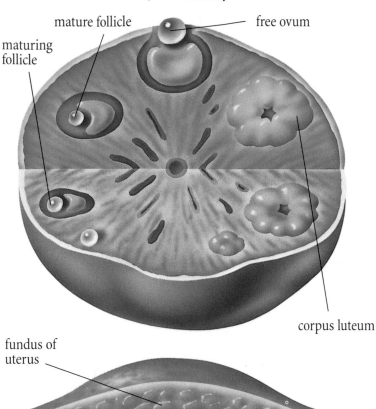

mature follicle

free ovum

maturing follicle

corpus luteum

fundus of uterus

uterus

body of the uterus

cervical canal

cervix

vagina

vaginal wall

**Vulva.** The outermost part of the female reproductive system is the vulva. It has two pairs of labia (labia majora and labia minora), flaps which cover the entrance to the vagina; and the clitoris, which is the sensory sexual organ. Between both pairs of labia lie Bartholin glands, which produce a lubricating fluid.

**Vagina.** The vagina is a muscular tube about 4-5 inches (10-12 cm) long that connects the uterus with the exterior. It is able to accept the penis during sexual intercourse. At the end of pregnancy, it forms the birth canal. The vagina consists of a mucous layer and a muscle layer. Cervical glands secrete a discharge inside the vagina that contains lactic acid. This acidifies the interior of the vagina to protect it from infections.

## UTERUS AND VAGINA
### (Cross section)

# The Ovum

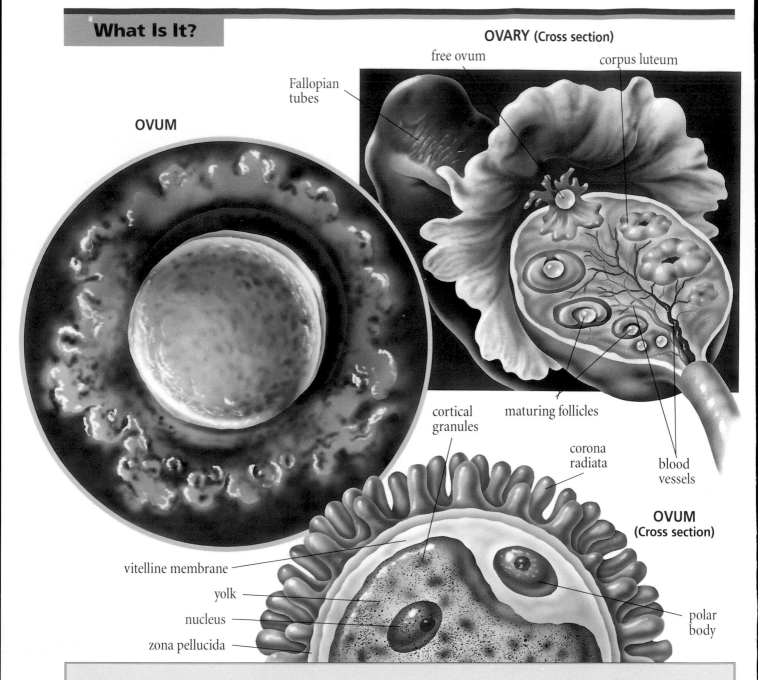

**OVUM**

**OVARY (Cross section)**

free ovum

corpus luteum

Fallopian tubes

cortical granules

maturing follicles

corona radiata

blood vessels

**OVUM (Cross section)**

vitelline membrane

yolk

nucleus

zona pellucida

polar body

**Production of female sex cells.** Each ovum is a spherical cell about 0.004 inch (0.1 mm) in diameter.

The ovum is surrounded by the corona radiata, formed from follicle cells. Beneath this is a thick, clear layer called the zona pellucida. Under this lies the actual cell wall, called the vitelline membrane. A spermatozoon needs to penetrate all these layers in order to fertilize the ovum. All spermatozoa carry an enzyme that will dissolve these membranes. The ovum's nucleus contains chromosomes.

Yolk is thinly scattered throughout the cytoplasm of the ovum. It nourishes the zygote, or fertilized ovum, through the first stages of growth.

The moment a spermatozoon penetrates the ovum, cortical granules in the ovum form a barrier that prevents entry by other spermatozoa. The ovum will survive only if it receives a spermatozoon within 24 hours after its release from the ovary. If it is not fertilized, the ovum disintegrates and is expelled from the uterus.

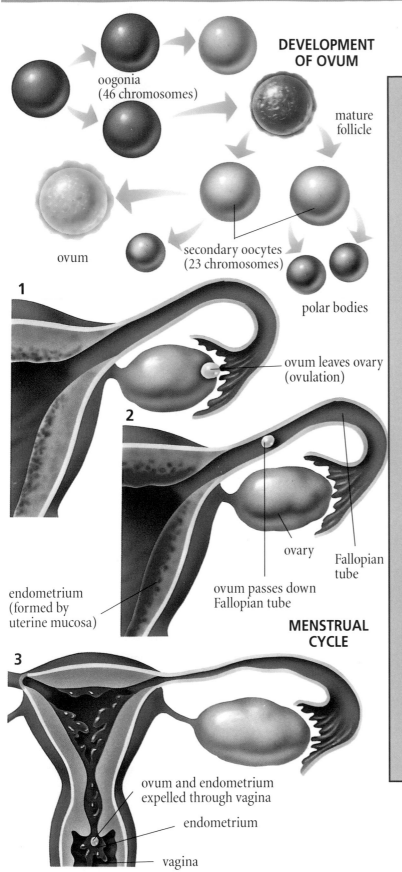

DEVELOPMENT
OF OVUM

oogonia
(46 chromosomes)

mature
follicle

ovum

secondary oocytes
(23 chromosomes)

polar bodies

1

ovum leaves ovary
(ovulation)

2

ovary

Fallopian
tube

endometrium
(formed by
uterine mucosa)

ovum passes down
Fallopian tube

MENSTRUAL
CYCLE

3

ovum and endometrium
expelled through vagina

endometrium

vagina

**Development of ovum.** The ovum is formed inside the follicles of the ovary during a two-stage process of meiosis: multiplication and maturation. During multiplication, germinal cells form oogonia, each containing 46 chromosomes, within ovarian follicles of 0.6-0.8 inch (1.5-2 cm) in diameter. The oogonia grow and change into primary oocytes within primary follicles.

Maturation starts at puberty. Primary oocytes divide into secondary oocytes with 23 chromosomes. In the next division, the secondary oocyte changes into an ovum. Each division also produces a polar body, a small nonfunctional cell that soon deteriorates. Every 28 days on average, a mature follicle ruptures, and the ovum leaves the ovary.

**Menstruation.** Ovulation occurs once a month. The ovum released from an ovary travels three or four days through the Fallopian tube toward the uterus. During this time, the ruptured follicle develops into a corpus luteum and begins to secrete progesterone, a hormone.

Progesterone prepares the endometrium for implantation of a fertilized ovum. If fertilization doesn't occur, progesterone production stops, and the spongy endometrium deteriorates and falls from the internal wall of the uterus. The ovum, blood, and tissue leave through the vagina. This menstruation process lasts from four to five days. Then, the cycle starts again.

# The Fertilization

**SPERMATOZOA PASSING THROUGH FALLOPIAN TUBE**

spermatozoa

Fallopian tube

ovum

**FEMALE REPRODUCTIVE SYSTEM**

uterus

gonads (ovaries)

external genitals

vagina

gonads (testicles)

spermatozoa

external genitals

ovum

**SPERMATOZOA APPROACHING OVUM**

**MALE REPRODUCTIVE SYSTEM**

**Producing new life.** All living beings reproduce so that a new generation can replace the previous one. For human reproduction, a fertilized ovum, or zygote, forms from the union of two cells, one male and one female. The genital, or reproductive, system produces reproductive cells or gametes. Although female and male reproductive systems are very different, both have gonads, genital tracts, and external genitals.

Gonads are the organs where gametes — spermatozoa in the male and ova in the female — are formed. The gonads also produce sex hormones, responsible for the external differences between male and female. The genital tracts are tubes that lead the gametes to the place where fertilization will take place. The external genitals are the organs that allow coitus, or sexual intercourse, to occur, during which female and male gametes meet. Fertilization consists of the union of the ovum and the spermatozoon to form a zygote, which is the first cell of a new human being.

In the human species, fertilization is an internal process — the male needs to introduce his spermatozoa into the female reproductive system. The spermatozoa swim at 0.12 inch (3 mm) per minute in a thirty-minute journey of 4 inches (10 cm). It is a passage with many hazards. For example, the secretion of the vaginal mucosa destroys 99 percent of the spermatozoa. Only the most robust survive.

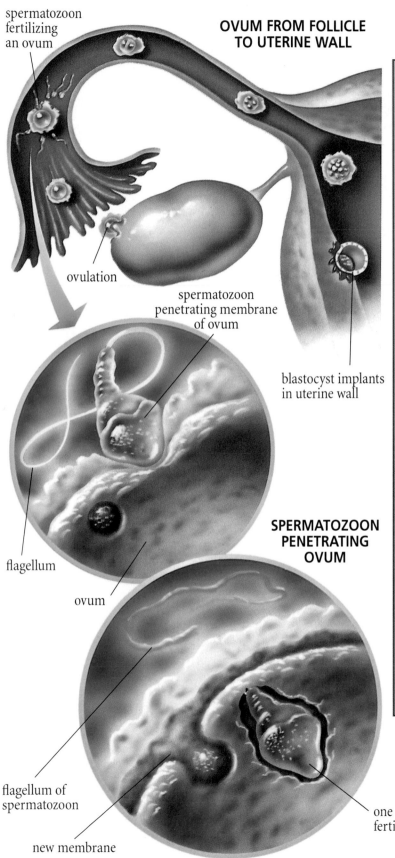

spermatozoon
fertilizing
an ovum

**OVUM FROM FOLLICLE
TO UTERINE WALL**

ovulation

spermatozoon
penetrating membrane
of ovum

blastocyst implants
in uterine wall

flagellum

ovum

**SPERMATOZOON
PENETRATING
OVUM**

flagellum of
spermatozoon

new membrane

one single spermatozoon
fertilizes the ovum

**Journey of the ovum.** Ovulation occurs when a follicle ruptures and expels an ovum. Cilia of the Fallopian tube fimbriae sweep the ovum inside, where it can be fertilized. To ensure fertilization, sexual union must take place within 24 hours after ovulation. After being fertilized, the zygote, now with 46 chromosomes, starts dividing while passing through the Fallopian tube. When it reaches the uterus, its cells have formed a hollow sphere called a blastocyst, which implants in the wall of the uterus, 7-8 days after fertilization. Here is where the embryo forms. The ruptured follicle becomes the corpus luteum, producing hormones to aid pregnancy in its first stages.

**Penetration.** Propelled by their whiplike flagella, spermatozoa arrive to gather around the ovum. Out of millions of spermatozoa that begin the journey, just a few thousand arrive at the upper Fallopian tube where fertilization takes place. Each contributes to the quantity of the enzyme needed to dissolve the protecting membranes of the ovum. Yet only one single spermatozoon will fertilize the ovum. At the moment of penetration, the ovum secretes a fertilization membrane that prevents other spermatozoa from entering. The spermatozoon's flagellum does not enter the ovum. Instead, it soon disintegrates.

# Glossary

**alimentary bolus** — a mass formed from food that has been chewed and mixed with saliva, ready to be swallowed.

**amylase** — an enzyme in the mouth and in the pancreas that breaks down starch to a simple sugar as part of the digestive process.

**chyme** — the liquid produced in the stomach by the mixing of food with gastric secretions.

**deciduous teeth** — the milk teeth, or first teeth, that erupt in humans between ages six months to eight months.

**dentin** — a bonelike substance of a tooth, forming the inner crown and the roots.

**embryo** — the fetus before the end of the third month of development inside the uterus.

**enzymes** — naturally occurring protein molecules that catalyze, or speed up, certain chemical reactions inside an organism.

**Fallopian tubes** — tubes leading from the ovary to the uterus through which the ovum travels.

**feces** — waste products formed after the digestion of food; excrements.

**fertilization** — the moment a spermatozoon penetrates an ovum, starting the development of a new organism.

**glomerulus** — the cluster of capillaries inside a nephron that filters fluid and wastes from blood.

**glycogen** — the stored form of glucose, especially occurring in the liver and muscles.

**gonad** — a reproductive gland; ovaries and testicles are gonads.

**hepatic lobule** — the tiny working unit of the liver where the exchange of substances between blood and liver takes place.

**hormone** — secretion from an endocrine gland that enters directly into the blood. The secretion affects the function of a particular organ.

**islets of Langerhans** — the endocrine portions of the pancreas that secrete insulin, which allows glucose to be changed into glycogen and stored in the liver and muscles as an energy source.

**lacteals** — the lymphatic capillaries in the villi of the small intestine that absorb the fatty end products of digestion.

**lipase** — an enzyme in pancreatic juice that breaks down fats into fatty acids and glycerol.

**mandible** — the lower jaw of mammals.

**maxilla** — the upper jaw of mammals.

**menstruation** — the process in the female in which the spongy tissue and blood vessels inside the uterus slough off and leave the body every 28 days on average.

**micron** — one-thousandth of a millimeter.

**mucosa** — tissues that cover the interior of body cavities; for example, the buccal mucosa covers the inside of the mouth.

**nephron** — the functional unit of the kidney that removes wastes from the blood and forms urine. It consists of the glomerulus, which filters blood, and the tubules, which reabsorb water and needed substances.

**oogenesis** — the process of cell division that produces an ovum in the ovary.

**ovum** — the female reproductive cell.

**pepsin** — an enzyme produced by the stomach that breaks down protein into smaller units called amino acids.

**peristalsis** — one-way, wavelike muscle contractions that propel substances through a hollow organ. Peristalsis moves the alimentary bolus down the esophagus.

**pharynx** — the space behind the mouth and nasal cavities and above the larynx and esophagus that forms a passage for air and food.

**protoplasm** — the inner living substance of a cell, including cytoplasm and the nucleus.

**puberty** — the stage of growth in humans when sexual maturity begins taking place, enabling the process of reproduction.

**rectum** — the last portion of the large intestine, just above the anus.

**saliva** — a mixture of water, mucin, protein, salts, and an enzyme that is secreted into the mouth by the salivary glands.

**scrotum** — the external skin pouch in the male between the upper thighs that contains the testicles.

**spermatogenesis** — the process in the testicles that produces spermatozoa.

**sphincter** — a ring-shaped muscle that opens and closes a cavity of the body.

**stomach** — the muscular pouch in which the process of digestion begins.

**testicle** — the male organ that produces spermatozoa and secretes testosterone.

**trypsin** — an enzyme produced by the pancreas that changes large amino acids into smaller ones.

**ureters** — the tubes that carry urine from the kidneys to the bladder.

**urethra** — the tube that carries urine from the bladder to outside the body.

**urinary system** — a system made up of the kidneys and the urinary ducts that filters the blood and retains water and waste to form urine.

**uterus** — the hollow, muscular organ in which the female carries a developing baby until it is born.

**villi** — folds of the mucosa in the small intestines, containing lacteals and capillaries, that absorb the products of digestion.

**zygote** — the cell resulting from the union of a male and a female reproductive cell.

# More Books to Read

*The Body. Young Scientist Concepts and Projects (series).* Steve Parker (Gareth Stevens)

*The Digestive System.* Regina Avraham (Chelsea House)

*Discovering the Whole You.* Joan Thiry (Chateau Thierry)

*Food and Digestion.* Jan Burgess (Silver Burdett Press)

*Life Before Birth.* Gary Parker (Master Books)

*The Living World. Record Breakers (series).* David Lambert (Gareth Stevens)

*Our Bodies. Under the Microscope (series).* Casey Horton (Gareth Stevens)

*Reproduction.* Jenny Bryan (Silver Burdett Press)

*The Reproductive System.* Regina Avraham (Chelsea House)

*The Reproductive System.* Alvin Silverstein, et al. (TFC Books)

# Videos to Watch

*I Am Joe's Kidney.* (Pyramid Media)

*I Am Joe's Liver.* (Pyramid Media)

*I Am Joe's Stomach.* (Pyramid Media)

*Menstruation: Hormones in Harmony.* (AGC Educational Media)

*Reproductive System.* (MTI Film and Video)

# Web Sites to Visit

ificinfo.health.org/brochure/10tipkid.htm

www.betterhealth.com/HK/ArticleMain/0,1349,169-475-200,00.html

www.betterhealth.com/HK/CategoryMain/0,1362,164-2034-,00.html

kidshealth.org/kid/

Some web sites stay current longer than others. For further web sites, use your browsers to locate the following topics: *anatomy, digestion, gallbladder, kidneys, liver, menstruation, reproduction,* and *teeth.*

# Index